GW00367993

WIND IN THE WILLOWS
BIRTHDAY BOOK

ISBN 0-86163-697-X

Copyright © 1993 Award Publications Limited

First published 1993 by Award Publications Limited
Goodyear House, 52-56 Osnaburgh Street, London NW1 3NS

Printed in Singapore

WIND IN THE WILLOWS
BIRTHDAY BOOK

Illustrated by Rene Cloke

AWARD PUBLICATIONS LIMITED

JANUARY

1 _____

_____

_____

2 _____

_____

_____

3 _____

_____

_____

JANUARY

"Come inside my dear fellow," Toad said. *"You too, Ratty."*

JANUARY

4

5

6

7

JANUARY

8

9

10

11

Mr. Toad and his friends often walked in the Wild
Wood.

JANUARY

12

13

14

15

JANUARY

16

17

18

JANUARY

19

20

21

22

JANUARY

Toad began to whistle a merry tune as he hopped and skipped along.

JANUARY

23

24

25

26 It is Mannette's
Birthday

JANUARY

27

28

29

30

JANUARY

31

Soon there wasn't a sound to be heard except for Mole's soft little snuffling snores!

FEBRUARY

1 _____

_____

_____

2 _____

_____

_____

3 _____

_____

_____

The door opened and
there was old Mr. Badger,
a lighted candle in his
hand.

FEBRUARY

4

5

6

7

FEBRUARY

Smiling broadly, Toad began scrambling down the window as quickly as he could with reckless speed.

8

9

10

FEBRUARY

11

12

13

14

FEBRUARY

15

16

17

18

FEBRUARY

19

20

21

22

23

24

25

FEBRUARY

"I'm coming too," said Otter. *"I know this wood.
I'll lead the way!"*

FEBRUARY

26

27

28

29

MARCH

1

2

3 Mummys Birthday
9597199 Mill Hill Parkside
N.W.7 2 LJ

Mole was delighted when his new friend Mr. Badger
lit his lantern and gave him a conducted tour all
over his house.

MARCH

4

5

6

7

"Cheer up, Mole, we'll turn back at once," said Ratty, as he took Mole's paw.

8

9

Mole took a lantern from a nail in the wall and struck a match. And there it was – the front door of his own house!

"There it is," said Mole. "We're home!"

MARCH

10

11

12

13

MARCH

14

15

16

17

18

_____

_____

_____

19

_____

_____

_____

_____

20

21

22

MARCH

23

24

25

26

MARCH

27

28

29

30

31

When the notes were ready one of the weasels acted as postman!

APRIL

1 _____

_____

_____

2 _____

_____

_____

3 _____

_____

_____

APRIL

"You may take the car back, my good man," said Badger as he addressed the delivery man.

APRIL

4

5

6

7

APRIL

8

9

10

APRIL

By nature Mole was a very quiet animal. The battle quite changed him and he went round collecting all the rifles the weasels and ferrets had left behind. He even asked Badger if he could keep one for himself.

APRIL

11

12

13

14

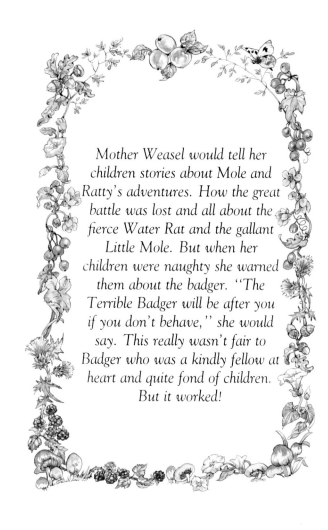

Mother Weasel would tell her
children stories about Mole and
Ratty's adventures. How the great
battle was lost and all about the
fierce Water Rat and the gallant
Little Mole. But when her
children were naughty she warned
them about the badger. "The
Terrible Badger will be after you
if you don't behave," she would
say. This really wasn't fair to
Badger who was a kindly fellow at
heart and quite fond of children.
But it worked!

15

16

17

18

19

20

21

22

APRIL

23

24

25

26

27

28

29

30

"Just listen to him," Mole whispered, as they stood outside his door. "He's made up a poem all about himself . . ."

MAY

1 _____

_____

_____

2 _____

_____

_____

3 _____

_____

_____

Toad made his boastful speech to the empty chairs in his room and felt all the better for it!

4

5

6

MAY

7

8

9

10

MAY

11

12

13

14

"Horray! How splendid! I was just going to send for you Ratty!" cried Toad as he caught sight of his friends.

15

16

The guards stood ready, waiting for the attack.

17

MAY

18

19

20

21

MAY

22

"Look, there he is!" Ratty cried suddenly.

MAY

23

24

25

26

27

28

29

30

MAY

31

Toad soon forgot to be jealous as he told his story.

"It would be nice if you could meet Toad," Water Rat exclaimed. And he scrambled to his feet and began waving frantically, making all kinds of signals to Toad to come ashore.

JUNE

1

2

3

JUNE

4

5

6

7

JUNE

8

9

10

11

JUNE

12

13

14

JUNE

15

16

17

18

JUNE

19

20

21

22

JUNE

Otter had seen a big fat mayfly, and with scarcely a splash, he dived into the water after it.

JUNE

23

24

25

26

JUNE

27 Sarahs Birthday
959 7199 Parkside MILLHILL
NW7 2LJ

28

29

30

It was one of the best days
of his life! There was so
much to eat he didn't
know what to try
first . . .

JULY

1 _____

_____

_____

2 _____

_____

_____

3 _____

_____

_____

_____

JULY

4

5

6

7

8 _____

_____

_____

9 _____

_____

10 _____

_____

_____

JULY

11

12

13

14

JULY

15

16

17

18

19

20

JULY

21

22

23

24

JULY

25

26

Mole was so happy that he sang a little song as he made his way along the side of the hedge, and he did a little dance.

27

28

29 Daniels Birthday
Mill Hill Park side
959 7199 NW7 2LJ

30

31

AUGUST

1

2

3

"I've never been in a boat before," Mole confessed,
as he climbed in.

4

In a surprisingly short time, Toad had harnessed the old horse he kept in the field and they were off!

AUGUST

5

6

7

8

AUGUST

9

10

11

12

13 _____

_____

_____

14 _____

_____

_____

_____

AUGUST

15

16

17

18

AUGUST

19

20

21

22

Toad went to look at the motor car. It was magnificent! It was everything a great car should be.

AUGUST

23

24

25

26

AUGUST

27

28

29

30

31

___

And how pleasant it was when night fell, to stop and have supper sitting on the grass by the side of the caravan.

SEPTEMBER

1 _____

_____

_____

2 _____

_____

_____

3 _____

_____

_____

Mole spluttered and choked as the water closed over his head. But Ratty was a fine swimmer and went to his rescue, bringing him to the bank.

Then he dived into the river again to recover the boat and fish up the basket.

SEPTEMBER

4

5

6

7

"You had better sit down," Ratty said at last, "and tell me why you are dressed in that ridiculous outfit . . ."

8

9

10

11

SEPTEMBER

12

13

14

15

SEPTEMBER

Clutching his bundle of washing, Toad made his way through the castle. His heart was beating so fast he thought the sentry must hear it.

SEPTEMBER

16

17

18

19

20

21

22

23

Mole was busy whitewashing his walls.

24

25

26

27

28

29

Rat and Mole shared their breakfast with two young hedgehogs who had called to see badger.

After a really wonderful supper Mr. Badger took
Ratty and Mole into his storeroom where he kept his
spare beds.

OCTOBER

1

2

3

OCTOBER

4

5

6

7

OCTOBER

8

9

Otter was another unexpected visitor. "So there you both are!" he cried, bursting into the room.

OCTOBER

Pushing his way to the head of the queue, he asked for a ticket to the nearest village to Toad hall.

OCTOBER

10

11

12

13

OCTOBER

14

15

16

17

*But when he got to the
front gate a big yellow ferret
with a gun fired at him and Toad
fell flat on his face.*

18 _____

_____

_____

19 _____

_____

_____

_____

20

_____

_____

_____

21

_____

_____

_____

OCTOBER

22

23

24

25

OCTOBER

26

27

28

29

OCTOBER

30

31

NOVEMBER

1 _____

_____

_____

2 _____

_____

_____

3 _____

_____

_____

As he sat in front of the roaring fire, with a mug of warm milky tea in his hand, Mole felt completely at home. He said as much to Ratty who immediately began making plans for the next day.

4

5

6

7

8

9

10

11

When Mole arrived the three friends talked together.

NOVEMBER

12

13

14

15

16

17

NOVEMBER

18

19

20

21

NOVEMBER

"The trap door," Badger hissed. "Now lads, heave away – all together. . ."

The heavy door creaked open and after a scramble they found they were in the pantry.

NOVEMBER

22

23

24

25

NOVEMBER

26

27

28

29 Ians birth day 9597199
Mill Hill NW7 2LJ
PARK side. Marks
Birthday 958 5H 35.

NOVEMBER

30

It was only when Ratty went to look outside that he was suddenly aware, for the first time, of Mole's tracks.

Rat and Mole set to work on the snow bank and
presently they came upon a solid little green
door and beside it a brass plate which read
MR. BADGER.

DECEMBER

1

2

3

4

5

*It was snowing hard.
Mole had to sit down after
he tripped over the door-
scraper and hurt his foot!*

DECEMBER

6

7

8

9

10

_____

_____

_____

11

_____

_____

_____

12

_____

_____

_____

13

_____

_____

_____

*Nearly all the guests
had managed to find
something smart to wear.*

14

15

16

17

DECEMBER

18

19

20

21

The fieldmice
carol singers made
a merry sight as
they trooped in and
formed a circle
"Now then boys" said
their conductor,
lifting his baton.

22

DECEMBER

23

24

25

26

27

28

29

30

DECEMBER

31

After the mice had sung one or two of Ratty's
favourite carols, he told them all to sit on Mole's big
settee – it was a tight squeeze! And there was a lot
of pushing and giggling.